A Christmas Carol

A Graphic Revision Guide for GCSE English Literature

Elizabeth May

Brilliant
PUBLICATIONS

We hope you and your pupils enjoy using the ideas in this book. Brilliant Publications publishes many other books to help teachers. To find out more details on any of the titles listed below, please go to our website: www.brilliantpublications.co.uk.

By the same author:
The Strange Case of Dr Jekyll and Mr Hyde: A Graphic Revision Guide for GCSE English Literature
Great Expectations: A Graphic Revision Guide for GCSE English Literature
Jane Eyre: A Graphic Revision Guide for GCSE English Literature
Pride and Prejudice: A Graphic Revision Guide for GCSE English Literature

Other titles which may be of interest:
How to Dazzle at Macbeth
How to Dazzle at Romeo and Juliet

Published by:
Brilliant Publications Limited
Unit 10, Sparrow Hall Farm, Edlesborough , Dunstable
Bedfordshire, LU6 2ES, UK
www.brilliantpublications.co.uk

EU Authorised Representative:
Easy Access System Europe
Mustamäe tee 50, 10621 Tallinn, Estonia
easproject.com
gpsr.requests@easproject.com

Brilliant Publications is a registered trademark.

Written and illustrated by Elizabeth May
Cover design by Brilliant Publications Limited

© Text and illustrations Elizabeth May 2019
© Design Brilliant Publications Limited 2019

Print   ISBN 978-0-85747-801-6
PDF   ISBN 978-0-85747-802-3

First printed and published in the UK in 2019. Printed and bound by CPI Group (UK) Ltd, Croydon, CR0 4YY

Contents

Introduction 4
How will this book be effective? 5

Visual chapter summaries

Stave 1: Marley's Ghost 6
Stave 2: The First of the Three Spirits 8
Stave 3: The Second of the Three Spirits 10
Stave 4: The Last of the Spirits 12
Stave 5: The End of It 14

Context and genre

Context 16
Genre: Folk Tale 17
Genre: Ghost Story 18
Genre: Social Commentary 19

Character profile pages

Scrooge 20
Bob Cratchit 21
Tiny Tim 22
Marley's Ghost 23
Ghost of Christmas Past 24
Ghost of Christmas Present 25
Ghost of Christmas Yet to Come 26
Ignorance and Want 27
More Characters: Fred, Belle, Fan, Fezziwig ... 28
More Cratchits and the Criminals 29

Theme pages

What is a theme? 30
Theme: Christmas 31
Theme: Time 32
Theme: Society 33
Theme: Loneliness 34
Theme: Change 35

Reference sheets

Christmas Day in London 36
Christmas with the Cratchits 37
Scrooge: before and after … 38

Activity pages

Vocabulary 39
Vocabulary: things & objects 40
Who is being described? 41
Which place is being described? 42
Who said it? 43
How would you feel if… 44
Trump cards 45
Character activity page 46
Quote analysis 47

Introduction

In GCSE English Literature there are long and complicated plots to follow and concepts to grasp that can be overwhelming for any student. For SEN students in particular, the importance of visuals to aid learning can never be underestimated. Around 65 per cent of us prefer to acquire information visually, and all of us can benefit from having large amounts of complex information repackaged in a fun, engaging, and simple way.

This book contains photocopiable resources that will strengthen students' understanding of *A Christmas Carol* in a format that is easily accessible and highly visual. It is ideal for students who want to support their study of this iconic story, and teachers who want to support their lessons.

In this book, you will find *A Christmas Carol* re-told in comic form, guide pages to aspects of the story, illustrations, and activity pages. These will all help to strengthen understanding of plot, characters, quotes, themes and much more.

How will this book be effective?

Exam specifications

The major exam boards (AQA, Edexcel and OCR) all look for very similar things when judging a student's performance. Here are the key skills a student should demonstrate to increase their likelihood of a high score; alongside are the pages in the book most relevant to that skill:

Skill	Pages
Understand and analyse words, phrases and sentences in context.	39–43, 47
Explore plot, characterisation, settings and events.	6–15, 20–29, 36–38, 41–42
Talk about different themes.	30–35
Generate opinions on the text.	44–47
Support their point of view using quotes and knowledge about context.	16–35
Show how language, form and structure of the text shape its meaning.	6–15, 17–19, 39–40, 47

SEN

These resources are suitable for any level of study, but are specifically tailored to GCSE study. They are tailored to be accessible to students with special educational needs (SEN). To do this, the book uses the following criteria:

- A heavy focus on **visuals**: using visual aids to learn is an educational recommendation for the vast majority of SEN students. It helps students to remember, understand, get interested in, and create associations to the text.
- **Simple language** for greater accessibility.
- A focus on **vocabulary**: explaining and rephrasing tricky words.
- A focus on **plot comprehension**: one of the biggest unaddressed stumbling blocks for SEN students. Chapter summaries are condensed to include key events, and are image-based to help students remember what happened and consolidate a full picture of the plot.
- A focus on the **key quotes** in the book that all students are more likely to be able to comprehend and remember more easily.

Although this book has been created in order to be accessible for SEN students generally, here is how the book can benefit some different types of SEN specifically:

- Provides a large amount of visual aids (LDD, ASD, SLCN, PNI, ADD, Dyslexia).
- Uses clear language (ASD, SLCN).
- Uses vocabulary lists and aims to develop vocabulary (LDD, ASD, SLCN).
- Breaks things down into small steps – particularly plot (LDD, ASD, ADD).
- Uses a range of activities (LDD, ADD).
- Encourages forming an opinion on, and empathising with, characters (ASD, SLCN).
- Repeats specific images and quotes (SLCN, ASD, Dyslexia).

Key:
ADD – Attention Deficit Disorder
ASD – Autistic Spectrum Disorder
LDD – Learning Difficulties and Disabilities
PNI – Physical and Neurological Impairments
SLCN – Speech, Language and Communication Needs

Ebenezer Scrooge is working in his counting-house, at his firm, 'Scrooge and Marley'.

Scrooge's business partner, Marley, has been dead for seven years...

but Scrooge never removed Marley's name from the business.

So, it's just Scrooge and his clerk, Bob Cratchit, working in the counting-house. Bob works in a tiny room next to Scrooge's office, with the door kept open so that Scrooge can check he is working hard.

Tonight, Bob is feeling cold, but Scrooge won't give him any coal for his fire.

All of a sudden, Scrooge hears a familiar voice.

It's Fred, Scrooge's nephew!

Fred tries to explain the joy he finds in Christmas, but Scrooge won't listen, so Fred soon leaves.

On his way out, Fred lets two gentlemen in.

Scrooge does not want to donate to the poor.

The weather gets colder, and a boy starts to sing a carol through the counting-house's keyhole.

Scrooge angrily scares the boy off.

Bob gets ready to go.

Scrooge agrees to let Bob have Christmas day off.

Scrooge eventually goes home too.

When Scrooge gets to the front door of his house, he sees something impossible…

his door knocker seems to have Marley's face in it!

But as Scrooge stares at the face…

it becomes a knocker again.

Scrooge goes inside, feeling nervous.

He checks all the rooms in the house.

Finally, he goes into his bedroom….

He makes sure to double-lock the door.

Scrooge sits down…

and then a bell in his room starts to ring by itself!

Scrooge hears the sound of clattering chains.

And then, in front of him, the ghost of Marley appears!

Scrooge can't believe what he is seeing.

He talks to the ghost, but is secretly terrified.

Scrooge starts saying that the ghost is not real.

Marley's ghost is so furious that Scrooge is refusing to believe he is real that he scares Scrooge by undoing his bandage and screaming.

This terrifies Scrooge!

Marley's ghost continues:

The ghost shows Scrooge a sky full of miserable spirits like him.

Then Scrooge falls asleep.

A Christmas Carol: A Graphic Revision Guide for GCSE English Literature

Scrooge wakes up in his bed.
Marley's ghost! Was it a dream? I don't think it was...
Marley said *three spirits* are going to come!

The clock strikes one.

A hand draws back Scrooge's bed curtain.

It's the first spirit – face-to-face with Scrooge!
Ghost of Christmas Past
For your welfare.
Why are you here, spirit?

The ghost takes Scrooge's hand and leads him into a field.
Wait...I know this place from my childhood!
Yes, you do! But for many years, you forgot all about it.

In a school building nearby, they find Scrooge as a young boy.
That's me! All alone on Christmas day. Ah...this makes me regret scaring off that carol-singing boy...

The vision changes – the room, and Scrooge, are suddenly older. This Christmas, Scrooge has a surprise visitor.
Fan!
Brother! Come home for Christmas!
My sister!
Fan
Yes, a lovely person she was. She died a woman.
Scrooge and the ghost talk about Fan and her son – Scrooge's nephew – Fred.

The Ghost of Christmas Past takes Scrooge to a different place, during a different Christmas time.

They go inside a warehouse where Scrooge is working as a young apprentice.
This is where I used to work.
Dick Wilkins

Scrooge's old boss walks in and tells them:
Let's finish early today! It's Christmas Eve, after all!
Hooray!
Fezziwig

Fezziwig starts a Christmas
Eve party in the warehouse!

The ghost takes them to
another Christmas scene.

They see Scrooge and a
woman in a discussion.

Scrooge recognises
her straight away – she
was his fiancée.

They watch as Belle breaks
up with Scrooge.

Scrooge is upset.

The ghost takes them to
another Christmas, which
was seven years ago, where
they see Belle talking to her
husband.

Scrooge really wants to go back
now. When he looks at the
ghost's face, he sees parts of all
the faces he was shown in the
visions of Christmas past.

He tries to get rid of
the ghost by putting its
extinguisher-cap on its
head, but its light only gets
stronger.

The next thing Scrooge
knows, he is asleep.

A Christmas Carol: A Graphic Revision Guide for GCSE English Literature

Scrooge wakes up.

The clock strikes 1am and Scrooge expects a ghost to appear…but it doesn't.

He gets up to explore, and hears a voice call him:

He follows the voice into the next room, only to see an extraordinary sight.

It's another spirit! This one is a jolly giant, sitting on a throne made of food, surrounded by Christmas decorations.

The spirit tells Scrooge to hold onto his robe.

He takes Scrooge to a busy city street on the morning of Christmas Day.

The weather isn't great, but everyone is filled with Christmas cheer.

And for anyone who isn't feeling jolly, the Ghost sprinkles some magic dust upon them from his torch, and they are jolly again.

The Ghost leads Scrooge into the suburbs.

They go into the house belonging to Scrooge's clerk, Bob Cratchit, his son Tiny Tim and all his family.

They are enjoying a lovely Christmas meal.

Then, Bob tries to toast Scrooge.

But Bob's family get upset when they hear Scrooge's name – none of them like him.

The Ghost transports them to an empty moor.

He shows Scrooge that even the miners, who live far away from everyone else, are celebrating Christmas.

The Ghost then transports them to a ship out in the ocean.

Inside, the sailors are also celebrating Christmas.

Deep in thought about the loneliness of the sea, Scrooge hears a familiar laugh.

It's Fred's laugh!

The Ghost has transported them to Fred's house, where he is talking about Scrooge with his wife and friends.

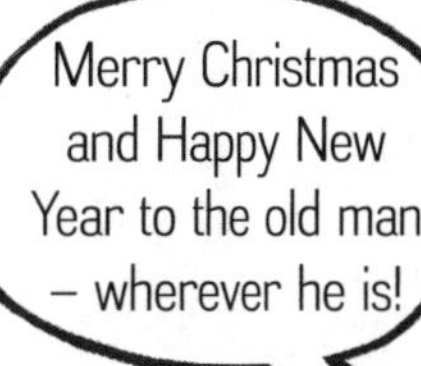

Fred and his friends have a lovely Christmas together, with music and games.

Scrooge plays along with the games, forgetting that no-one can hear him.

Fred wishes Scrooge a merry Christmas.

After a while, Scrooge notices the Ghost has become older.

Scrooge notices something under the Ghost's robe.

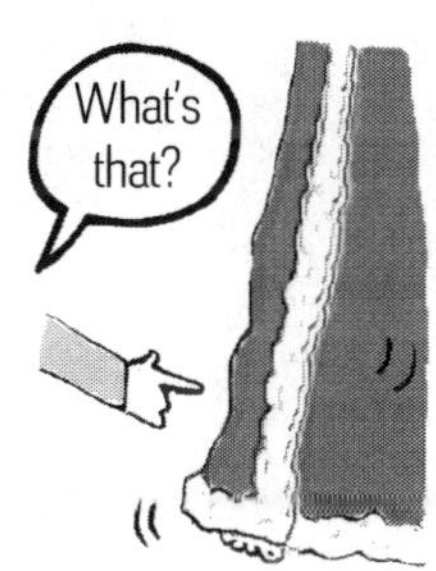

From under its robe, the Ghost reveals two scrawny, neglected children. He says they belong to mankind. Scrooge is shocked.

The Ghost echoes Scrooge's earlier words about the poor.

The clock then strikes twelve, and the Ghost disappears....

Then the Ghost of Christmas Yet to Come silently and slowly approaches Scrooge.

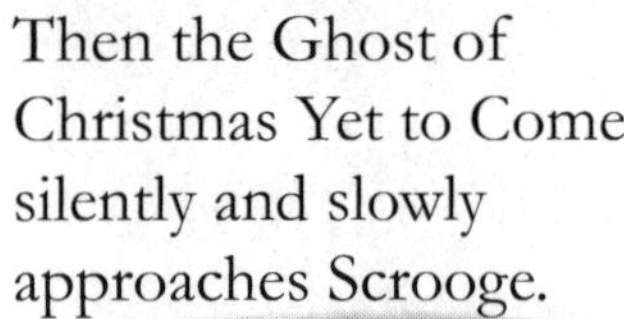
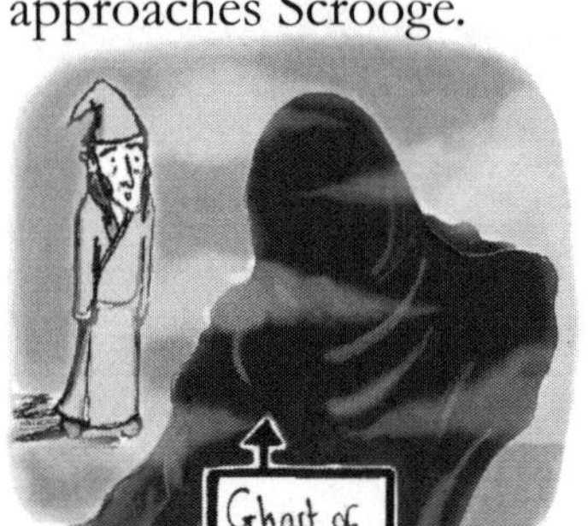

It's a scary spirit that does not talk, it only points.

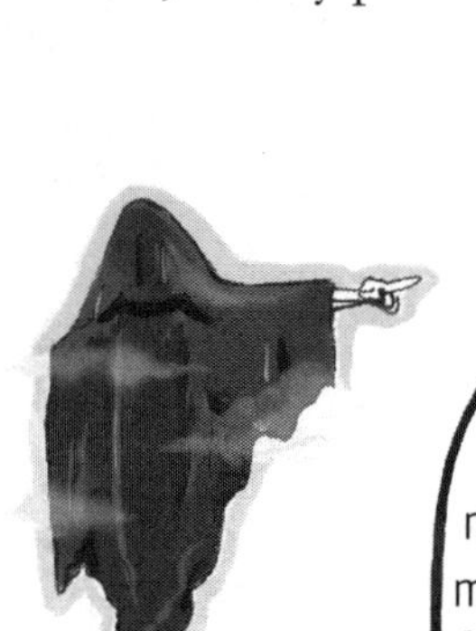

The Ghost whisks Scrooge away into a street where a group of men are talking.

The Ghost then takes Scrooge to two more gentlemen who stop for a quick chat.

The Ghost leads Scrooge to a run-down, dirty part of the city.

They go to a pawn shop, where a group of people discuss some things they found and want to sell.

The Ghost takes Scrooge to a dark room with a bed. There is a body under the cover.

The Ghost points to the body, as if to ask Scrooge to uncover it.

The Ghost does as Scrooge asks, and they look upon a family.

So it turns out the only emotion felt because of the man's death was *happiness*....

The Ghost obeys. It takes Scrooge to the Cratchit house, where Tiny Tim has just died.

The Ghost leads Scrooge somewhere.

and into a graveyard.

Scrooge is too scared to look at the name on the headstone.

They go past Scrooge's old office…

The Ghost points to a headstone.

The Ghost does not answer; it only points to the headstone…

and then to Scrooge!

Scrooge pleads with the Ghost…

but it has gone.

Scrooge becomes aware that he is in bed.

He is filled with a desire to become a better person.

Scrooge talks to himself. He is overcome with joy.

Scrooge goes to his window, opens it and looks out at a glorious, sunny day.

He asks a boy on the street what the day is.

Scrooge is so happy to learn that he hasn't missed Christmas.

He asks the boy a favour.

The boy returns with the turkey.

Scrooge gets dressed and shaved.

Scrooge goes out onto the streets, and wishes everyone he passes a merry Christmas. Then, he comes across one of the gentlemen who asked him for money to help the poor yesterday.

Scrooge goes about his Christmas day happily. He goes to church…

enjoys talking to people…

and enjoys a walk.

Then, he decides to take up Fred's offer from yesterday, and join him and his family for dinner.

Scrooge is nervous about knocking on the door…

but eventually he builds up the courage.

Fred is delighted to see Scrooge.

Fred's family welcome Scrooge warmly.

They have a wonderful Christmas together!

The next morning…

Scrooge gets into work early and waits for Bob.

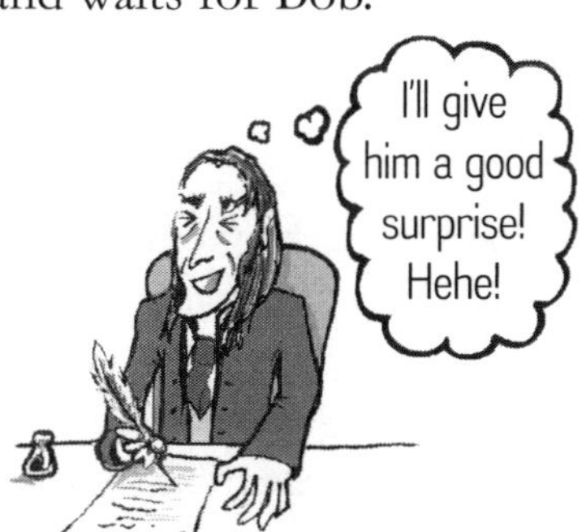

Bob comes in eighteen and a half minutes late. Scrooge pretends to be angry about this.

In the future…

Scrooge has truly changed his ways.

Scrooge becomes a great, friendly man who was known throughout the city for his love of Christmas.

He becomes like a second father to Tiny Tim – who did not die!

Context

19th century England

Time: *A Christmas Carol* was written and published in **1843**. Although the exact time Dickens **set** the story is unclear, it is likely to be around the same time.

Place: **London**, the capital city of England.

In the 19th century, England was going through the **Industrial Revolution**: a time when people started making, selling and buying things much more than before. Many people moved to cities to work in factories for small amounts of money, so cities became **overcrowded.** This led to more **poverty** and **homelessness**. Politicians wanted to help solve this problem, so they passed **The Poor Law Amendment Act**, which sent the poor to horrible **workhouses.** Dickens noticed that the middle and upper classes did not seem to care about the lives of the poor, and this upset him: he said that London was a 'hopeless nursery of **ignorance**, **misery** and **vice'**.

The 19th century was also a time when Christmas traditions, like carol singing , trees and cards, became more popular. Much of this new popularity was due to the Victorian Royal Family's love of Christmas, which the public wanted to follow.

Charles Dickens

Dickens had moved in and out of London with his family throughout his childhood. At age 12, he had to work in a **factory** for 10 hours a day to help earn money for his family. Dickens hated working – but this experience was important for him in forming his opinions on **society** and the **poor**. He was later sent to school, and at age 15 he started to work as a law clerk, then later a journalist and writer.

Dickens wrote *A Christmas Carol* in 1843. He had recently visited a London **'ragged school'**, where homeless and poor children went to learn for free. Dickens felt sorry for the children he saw there and wanted more money to be put into ragged schools. He wanted to write informational pamphlets for the public to read about these schools so more people could think about how they could **help** poor children – but he decided to write *A Christmas Carol* to encourage people to think about the situation instead.

GENRE:
Folk Tale

A Christmas Carol **could be considered to fit into the 'folk tale' genre because it has the following elements:**

- **Supernatural elements**: The three spirits and Marley's ghost all play crucial roles in the story.

- **Easily retold**: The story is short and fast-paced. Dickens often did public Christmas readings of *A Christmas Carol*, which were popular with Victorian crowds.

- **A hero and a villain**: Interestingly, Scrooge could be both of these. This is because by the end of the story, he helps to 'save' Tiny Tim and the Cratchits with his money, help and generosity. However, at the beginning of the story he fits the role of a villain: selfish, unkind and greedy.

- **Rule of Three**: In many folk tales, events or characters come in sets of three (e.g. Goldilocks and the Three Bears). This gives the story a repetitive, memorable structure. In *A Christmas Carol*, we see this element in the three spirits who visit Scrooge.

- **Good vs evil**: We see elements of 'evil' in Scrooge's character at the beginning, wherein he refuses to give to charity and has no regard for the feelings of others. Forces of 'good' appear as the spirits, the Cratchits and Fred.

- **A character learning a lesson**: At the end of the story, Scrooge has learned kindness and generosity from the spirits, and has changed his ways completely.

The effect of the 'folk tale' aspects of *A Christmas Carol* is that its message of kindness and generosity to the poor is easily accessible to everyone. It is a short, enjoyable story that people can easily remember and re-tell, with a strong and clear 'moral of the story'.

GENRE:
Ghost Story

A Christmas Carol **could be considered to fit into the 'ghost story' genre because it has the following elements:**

✓ **Meant to be told out loud to an audience**: Dickens would often read the story aloud to large crowds at Christmas.

✓ **Told to entertain**: The story is fast-paced, eventful and dramatic.

✓ **Scares the audience**: The story is full of ghosts, as well as the scary prospects of loneliness and eternal suffering after death if you don't live life well. Dickens' middle and upper class audiences may have felt scared about their own fates after hearing the story.

✓ **A focus on the supernatural**: The spirits are a big part of the story.

✓ **Strange weather**: On Christmas Eve it is foggy and bleak; when the Ghost of Christmas Past shows up, it is 'well below freezing'; when the Ghost of Christmas Present shows Scrooge a vision of present-day Christmas, the weather is 'severe'. However, when the visions are over and Scrooge wakes up on Christmas Day, the cold and fog is all gone, and there is 'golden sunlight'.

The 'ghost story' genre fits well into the story as it helps to carry its message of charity and generosity: it makes Dickens' Victorian readers think about something they would usually avoid thinking about (the suffering of the poor), whilst being entertaining. It may also have scared people into being more generous!

GENRE:
Social Commentary

A Christmas Carol **could be considered to fit into the 'social commentary' genre because it has the following elements:**

 **Brings attention to a problem:** In Stave 1, Dickens makes sure to highlight Scrooge's selfishness and his lack of empathy towards the poor.

 **Makes people think about fairness:** By including the Cratchits in the story, readers are encouraged to think about how unfair it is that a good family faces poverty and death whilst Scrooge is rich and unkind. The characters Ignorance and Want also help readers to think about how unfair it is for children to be in poverty.

 **Encourages change:** By having Scrooge change his character completely by the end of the story, Dickens encourages his readers to be capable of change as well.

 **Reflects the context of the story:** Dickens set the story around the time that he wrote it (mid-19th century) so that readers would recognise modern social problems in the story.

 **Reflects the author's opinions:** Dickens himself was very passionate about helping the poor and changing wealth inequality, which is a major theme in the story.

Being a social commentary, the story is able to focus in on encouraging generosity and charity at a time of year that is all about giving to others and spending time with family.

SCROOGE

Full name: Ebenezer Scrooge
Also known as: 'the old man', 'old Scratch'

IMPORTANCE:

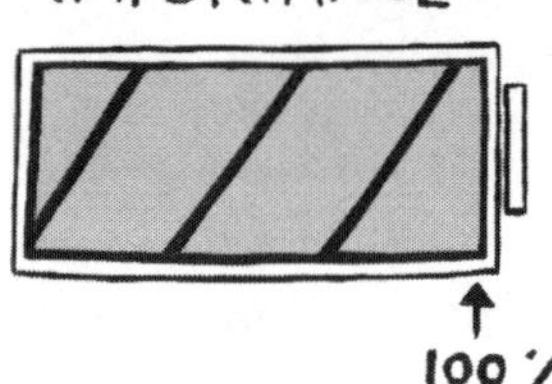

Fact file:

- Scrooge is a mean, lonely and miserable man at the beginning of the story. He only cares about money.
- Scrooge had some difficult times in his life which might have made him like this, such as losing his sister, spending most of his childhood away from home, and losing his business partner…
- However, he often brings loneliness on himself by rejecting others, like his nephew, Fred.
- Throughout the story, Scrooge slowly learns the joy of Christmas and the importance of kindness and generosity.
- At the end of the story, Scrooge is forever changed. He is a good, kind man who loves Christmas.

Appearance:
Scrooge has 'old features', a 'pointed nose', a 'shrivelled cheek' and 'ferret eyes'. He has red eyes, blue lips and a stiff way of walking, which, Dickens writes, comes as a result of 'the cold within him'.

What people say about him:

BOB CRATCHIT

Also known as: The clerk, Robert

Fact file:

- Bob works for Scrooge's firm, 'Scrooge and Marley', as the clerk. This means he is like an office worker.
- He has a large family but struggles to provide for them as Scrooge pays him a very low salary.
- He is always grateful to Scrooge even though he has a difficult life and is treated unfairly by Scrooge.
- At the beginning of the story, he is like the opposite of Scrooge: happy, optimistic, social and loving.

IMPORTANCE:

80%

Appearance:
Bob looks 'shabby', as his clothes are old and 'threadbare'. He wears a 'white comforter', which is like a scarf, to keep him warm. The narrator often calls him 'little Bob', suggesting he is short and thin.

What people say about him:

A Christmas Carol: A Graphic Revision Guide for GCSE English Literature

TINY TIM

Full name: Tim Cratchit

Fact file:

- Tiny Tim is one of Bob Cratchit's children.
- He is disabled, and uses a crutch and an iron frame for support.
- Dickens may have been inspired by his nephew, Henry, to write Tiny Tim's character. Henry was also disabled.
- Tiny Tim is supposed to be read as a good and pure character because he is thoughtful and religious.
- The Ghost of Christmas Yet to Come shows Scrooge a future where Tiny Tim has died – possibly because the Cratchits were not rich enough to get him proper care…
- However, Tiny Tim does not die, and Scrooge becomes like a second father to him.

Appearance:
Tiny Tim is a 'little, little child' who 'bore a little crutch, and had his limbs supported by an iron frame'. The narrator refers to Tiny Tim's 'withered little hand', which suggests the rest of him is 'withered' too.

What people say about him:

As good as gold... and better. Somehow he gets thoughtful...and thinks the strangest things you ever heard. He told me, coming home, that he hoped the people saw him in the church, because he was a cripple, and it might be pleasant to them to remember upon Christmas Day, who made lame beggars walk, and blind men see.

Stave 3

I am sure we shall none of us forget poor Tiny Tim.

Stave 4

I know, my dears, that when we recollect how patient and how mild he was; although he was a little, little child; we shall not quarrel easily among ourselves, and forget poor Tiny Tim in doing it.

Stave 4

Spirit of Tiny Tim, thy childish essence was from God!

Stave 4

MARLEY'S GHOST

Also known as: The phantom, the Ghost, the spectre, the apparition, (Scrooge's) partner, Jacob

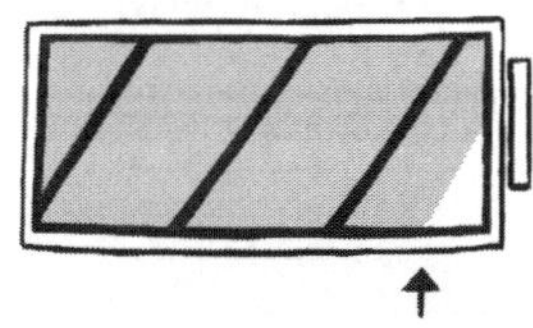

Fact file:

- Marley died on Christmas Eve exactly seven years before the story begins.
- He used to be Scrooge's business partner. Their firm was called 'Scrooge and Marley'.
- Marley's Ghost visits Scrooge on Christmas Eve to warn him that he is not living his life correctly, and that if he doesn't change, Scrooge will become a miserable spirit forever trapped in chains like him.
- Marley appears first as a face in Scrooge's door knocker, then later comes booming from the cellar into Scrooge's bedroom.

Appearance:
Marley's Ghost's face has a 'dismal light about it' and 'ghostly spectacles turned up on its ghostly forehead'. His eyes are 'wide open', 'motionless' and 'death cold'. He wears his 'usual waistcoat, tights, and boots', and has a 'folded kerchief bound about its head and chin'. He carries a chain made of 'cash-boxes, keys, padlocks, ledgers, deeds, and heavy purses wrought in steel.'

What people say about him:

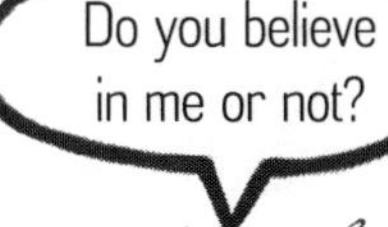

GHOST OF CHRISTMAS PAST

Also known as: 'the unearthly visitor', 'the Ghost', 'the Spirit'

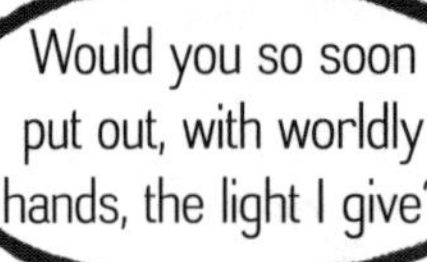

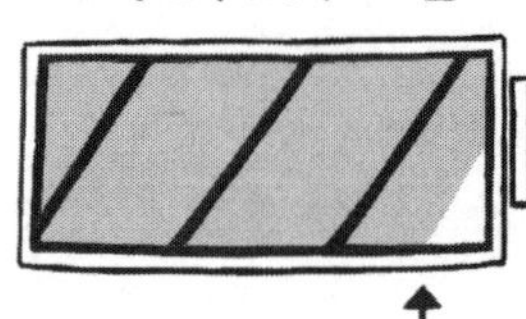

Fact file:

- The Ghost of Christmas Past is the first spirit to visit Scrooge after Marley's ghost disappears.
- This Spirit is strange, but kind and guiding towards Scrooge.
- It takes Scrooge to see various Christmases from his past.
- Scrooge struggles with seeing things from the past he would rather forget – particularly Belle breaking up with him – and tries to make the spirit leave by pushing its extinguisher-cap down on its head.

Appearance:

This spirit has long white hair, no wrinkles, and 'muscular' arms and hands. It wears '(pure) white' robes, a 'lustrous' belt, and flowers. From its head, 'there spring a bright clear jet of light', but different parts of it glow and sparkle, and go dark or disappear.

What people say about him:

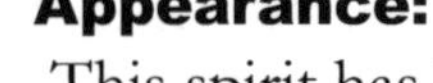

GHOST OF CHRISTMAS PRESENT

Also known as: the Phantom, the Ghost, the Spirit

Fact file:

- The Ghost of Christmas Present is the second spirit to visit Scrooge after Marley's ghost disappears.
- This spirit is a 'giant', but it can fit into any space.
- He tells Scrooge he has had 'more than eighteen hundred' brothers. Since *A Christmas Carol* was published in 1843, the spirit is saying that since the year AD 1, a 'Ghost of Christmas Present' has been born, and later died, on Christmas Day.
- The spirit takes Scrooge to lots of different places so he can see how all kinds of people celebrate Christmas at the same time.
- By the end of Stave 3, he appears old, and reveals two awful-looking children, 'Ignorance' and 'Want', from under his robe, to make Scrooge rethink the horrible things he said about poor people.

IMPORTANCE:

Appearance:
This spirit has 'clear and kind' eyes that sparkle. It has 'dark brown curls' that are 'long and free', and wears a 'holly wreath' on its head. The spirit is 'clothed in one simple green robe…bordered with white fur'. It has an 'antique scabbard', which is a case to hold a sword; but the scabbard is empty. The spirit gets older toward the end of the day it spends with Scrooge.

What people say about him:

GHOST OF CHRISTMAS YET TO COME

Also known as: 'the Phantom', 'the Spirit', 'the Ghost', 'Ghost of the Future', 'Spectre'

IMPORTANCE:

↑ 90%

Fact file:

- The Ghost of Christmas Yet to Come is the last spirit that visits Scrooge.
- The ghost never talks, and never shows its features. It communicates with Scrooge by pointing.
- It is an eerie, scary ghost, but Scrooge still describes it as 'good', and the narrator describes it as 'kind', because it is ultimately just trying to help Scrooge.

Appearance:
This spirit is 'shrouded in a deep black garment, which concealed its head, its face, its form'. All that you could see other than the spirit's cloak was 'one outstretched hand'.

What people say about him:

IGNORANCE and WANT.

Fact file:

* Ignorance and Want are both poor, neglected children that the Ghost of Christmas Present shows to Scrooge.
* They are both symbols that represent poverty, and what happens when people forget to help others, especially those less fortunate in society.
* Dickens wrote these characters as children to show that the unkind way society treated the poor had the worst effects on children: the most innocent and blameless members of society.
* In Stave 1, Scrooge says the poor should just go to 'prisons' or 'workhouses', but when he sees Ignorance and Want, he regrets what he said.

Appearance:
Ignorance and Want are a boy and a girl, both 'yellow, meagre, ragged, scowling (and) wolfish'. This means they are thin, hungry and dirty, and they almost look like wild animals. They look 'hideous' and 'miserable'.

What people say about them:

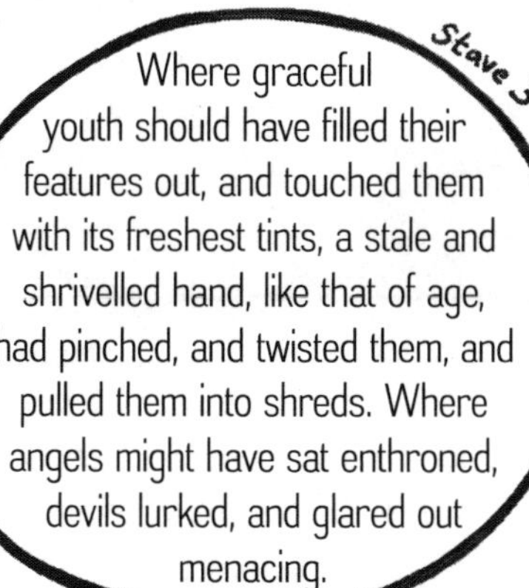

A Christmas Carol: A Graphic Revision Guide for GCSE English Literature

MORE CHARACTERS...

FRED

Fact file:
- Fred, who is Scrooge's nephew, loves Christmas and wants to involve Scrooge in the celebrations.
- Fred is an example of the sociable, generous type of person Dickens wants his readers to be.

BELLE

Fact file:
- Belle and Scrooge were engaged to be married in the past, but…
- Belle broke it off because she felt that Scrooge cared more about money than her.
- Scrooge is shown a vision of her in later life, with children and happily married.

FAN

Fact file:
- Fan is Scrooge's sister and Fred's mother, although we never meet her as an adult in the story.
- Fan and Scrooge were very fond of each other when they were young. Fan misses her brother when he has to go away for school.

FEZZIWIG

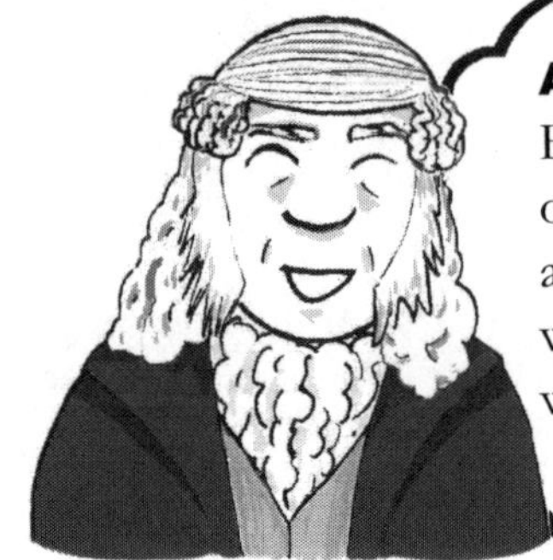

Fact file:
- When Scrooge was a young apprentice, Fezziwig was his boss.
- He has since died, so Scrooge is happy to see him in a vision.
- He was a good boss, making sure his workers were happy and letting them celebrate Christmas Eve.

MORE CRATCHITS

Alongside Bob and Tiny Tim, the Cratchit family consists of Mrs. Cratchit, who is Bob's wife, and their other children: Martha, Peter, Belinda, and 'two smaller Cratchits, a boy and a girl'. Dickens describes them as 'not a handsome family' and 'not well dressed'. He wanted the Cratchit family to be an example of a good, wholesome family that is poor and needs help and charity from others, to inspire his readers to be more charitable to the poor.

THE CRIMINALS

This gang of shady characters meet together in a 'low-browed, beetling shop' in a bad part of the city. The shop makes money from selling second-hand items, so Mrs. Dilber, the undertaker's man, and the charwoman have gone to Scrooge's house to steal all of his things and sell them once they found out he died. It is a vision shown to Scrooge by the Ghost of Christmas Yet to Come, to scare him into leading a better life so that people will care about his eventual death, unlike these criminals.

A Christmas Carol: A Graphic Revision Guide for GCSE English Literature

What is a Theme?

A theme is an **idea** that comes up **again** and **again**. The author will put themes in a book because they want the reader to **think** about certain things.

Themes carry **messages** and help to create an **effect** on the reader.

Here are some of the themes from *A Christmas Carol*:

Use the following pages to help you decide which themes link to each other, and see if you can think of any more. Remember – you can talk about themes in any exam question.

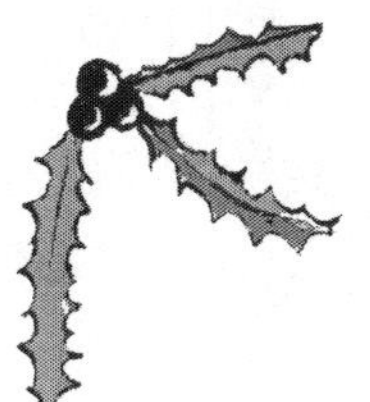
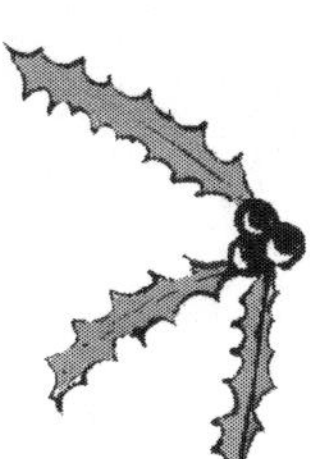

THEME: Christmas

In the 19th century, Christmas was becoming more popular than ever before. This was partly because Queen Victoria and her husband Albert were big fans of Christmas. It was Albert who brought the idea of Christmas trees to England!

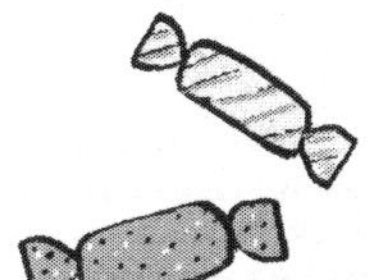

Christmas became a holiday that was centred around spending time with family. This links to other themes in the story around **society** and **loneliness** – Dickens wants the reader to think about Christmas as a time to spend with others, and remind us that Scrooge is missing out on one of the most important parts of Christmas by wanting to spend it alone.

The theme of Christmas was an important way for Dickens to relay his message of encouraging **kindness, generosity** and **sociability**, as Christmas is seen as a time for all of these things.

Quotes about Christmas:

Stave 1

...every idiot who goes about with 'Merry Christmas' on his lips, should be boiled with his own pudding, and buried with a stake of holly through his heart. He should!

Stave 1

I have made the trial in homage to Christmas, and I'll keep my Christmas humour to the last. So A Merry Christmas, uncle!

Stave 4

I will honour Christmas in my heart, and try to keep it all the year.

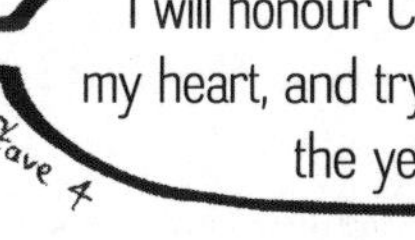

Stave 1

There are many things from which I might have derived good, by which I have not profited, I dare say... Christmas among the rest.

Stave 3

...it is good to be children sometimes, and never better than at Christmas, when its mighty Founder was a child himself.

A Christmas Carol: A Graphic Revision Guide for GCSE English Literature

THEME: Time

A Christmas Carol goes back and forth between different times, and the reader is therefore not sure of exactly where Scrooge is in his **timeline**. The story starts on Christmas Eve, but after Scrooge is visited by Marley's Ghost and falls asleep, it isn't clear to the reader whether Scrooge is dreaming, or really travelling backwards and forwards in time with the spirits – or both. This helps the reader feel Scrooge's **confusion** about what is happening to him.

Time is so important to the story because, as Scrooge gets older, he has less of a chance to **change his ways** and stop his fate being the same as Marley's – stuck forever as a miserable ghost in chains.

As the Ghost of Christmas Past takes Scrooge through his boyhood and into adulthood and beyond, we see Scrooge lose sight of the **important** things in life, like relationships. The Ghost of Christmas Present shows Scrooge that the people in his life do still appreciate him despite his mean and unkind ways; but the Ghost of Christmas Yet to Come shows that eventually, those who cared about Scrooge are pushed away entirely – nobody was sad to hear of him dying. This shows that as time passes, Scrooge loses out on the important parts of life, and if he wants to start changing his ways, it needs to be quick.

The past, present and future are very important themes in the book as they explore how the events in Scrooge's life all tie together. The spirits visit him to show him events from his life in chronological order. In this way, we see how the events in Scrooge's life all link together to create his **outcome**. It also encourages us as readers to reflect on our own lives, and think about how the **past** impacts on our **present** and **future**.

Quotes about Christmas:

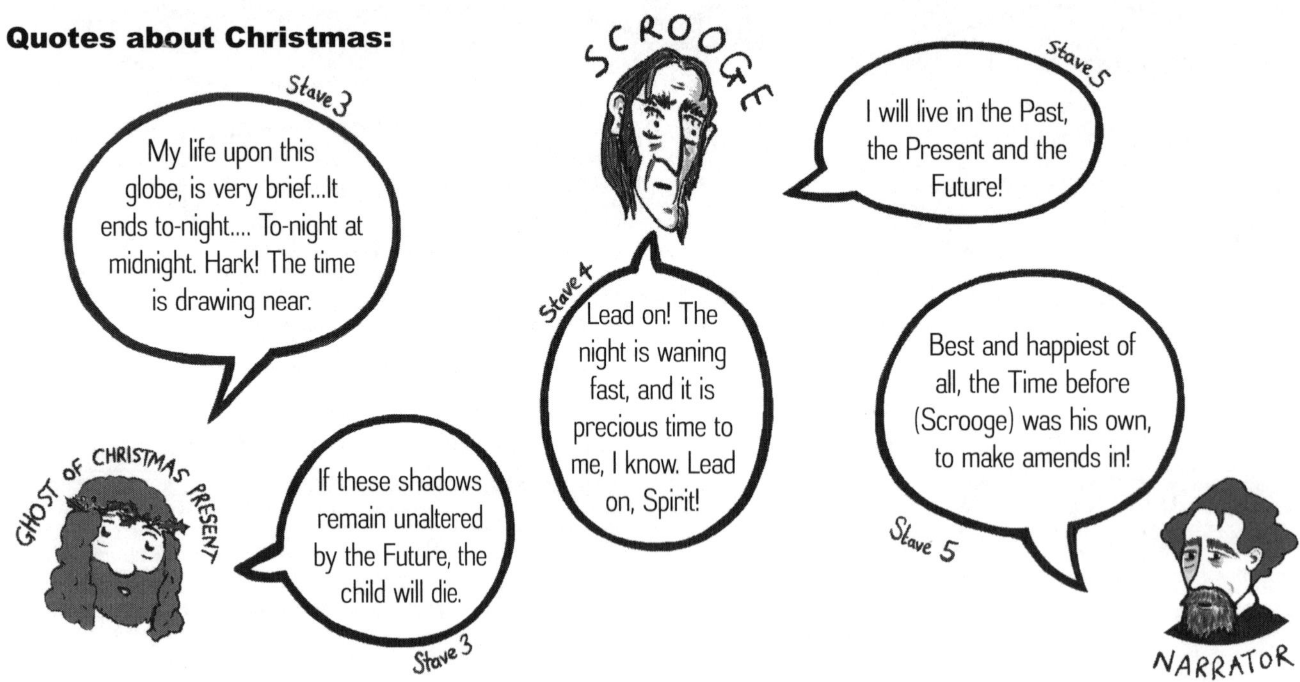

THEME:
Society

'Society' means the **people** that make up a **community** – for example, the people within a certain town, or within a family or group. In 19th century London, **inequality** was a big problem in society. This means that some people were more fortunate than others, and the type of inequality Dickens wants his readers to think about in particular is **wealth inequality**. There was a big difference in quality of life between the rich and the poor.

The struggles of people in poverty are important in the story of *A Christmas Carol*. In fact, Dickens wrote this story so that he could influence society to think about **helping the poor**. As the main character of the story, Scrooge represents the richer parts of society – people who see and interact with those in poverty (like the Cratchits) but don't care enough to help. By creating characters readers will feel sympathy towards (like Tiny Tim), and changing Scrooge's views about the poor, Dickens hopes to help society also feel sympathy towards the poor and start to help them more.

Quotes about society:

Stave 1

At this festive season of the year, Mr. Scrooge...it is more than usually desirable that we should make some slight provision for the Poor and destitute, who suffer greatly at the present time. Many thousands are in want of common necessaries; hundreds of thousands are in want of common comforts, sir.

Stave 1

It's enough for a man to understand his own business, and not to interfere with other people's.

Stave 1

Mankind was my business. The common welfare was my business; charity, mercy, forbearance, and benevolence, were, all, my business.

Stave 1

We choose this time, because it is a time, of all others, when Want is keenly felt, and Abundance rejoices.

A Christmas Carol: A Graphic Revision Guide for GCSE English Literature

Loneliness

As people celebrate and enjoy Christmas together, Scrooge is the only character we meet in the story who **chooses to be alone**. We see that Scrooge's loneliness in Stave 1 is his choice and preference, as he rejects Fred's offer to spend Christmas at his house. He also purposely **drives others away**: he is rude to the charity collectors, scares away a singing boy and makes no attempt to be kind to Bob.

When the Ghost of Christmas Past shows Scrooge visions from his childhood, however, we see that Scrooge experienced loneliness in the past not by choice. For example, he was **sent away** to boarding school by his father when he was a boy. Later, when they are adults, Scrooge becomes more lonely when his sister, Fan, dies.

From adulthood, Scrooge cares less and less about being lonely. When Belle breaks up with him, she says that he loves money more than he loves her, and Scrooge does not deny this. This is a characteristic that we see emerge in Scrooge over time: his view that **money** is more important than **people**. However, Scrooge sees the consequences of this in the Ghost of Christmas Yet to Come's visions, where his rejection of friends, family and society leads to nobody caring about his death.

Quotes about loneliness:

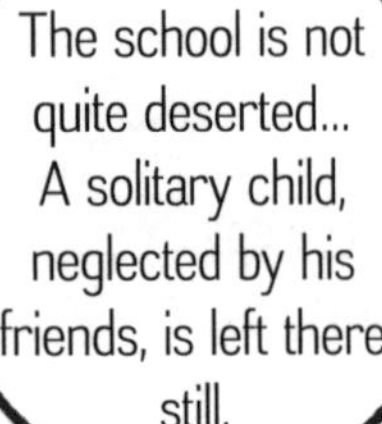

THEME: Change

Throughout the story, Scrooge undergoes a change as he is shown the error of his ways by the spirits, and sees how his behaviour impacts both others and himself.

By the end of the story, Scrooge is like a completely different man. In Stave 1 he is **mean, selfish** and **miserable**, but by Stave 5 he has become **happy** and **generous**.

Scrooge's **fate** also changes. In Stave 1, we find out from Jacob's ghost that those in life who live selfishly end up as miserable spirits in chains after they die. Worse than this, Jacob's ghost tells Scrooge that Scrooge's chain is already longer than his own. But there is a way to change this – Marley's ghost says Scrooge has a 'chance and hope of escaping (his) fate' if he listens to the three spirits that will visit him. By Stave 4, when the Ghost of Christmas Yet to Come shows Scrooge that nobody is affected by his death, Scrooge begs the ghost to tell him if he can **change the future** and stop this outcome. Waking up, he discovers that he can. Scrooge does end up learning the lesson from the spirits that Marley's ghost wanted him to learn, and does change his fate.

Quotes about change:

Christmas Day in London

Christmas with the Cratchits

Scrooge:
before
and
after

Vocabulary

Here are some words that come up in *A Christmas Carol* **that are important in the story.**

Word	Quote	Meaning
covetous	'(Scrooge was) a squeezing, wrenching, grasping, scraping, clutching, covetous old sinner!'	Greedy; wanting to buy and own a lot of things.
gain	'I have seen your nobler aspirations fall off one by one, until the master-passion, Gain, engrosses you.'	Getting and earning things.
humbug	'It's humbug still!…I won't believe it.'	A fraud; something that is fake.
idol	'Another idol has displaced me.'	Something that someone worships.
ignorance	'This boy is Ignorance.'	Not knowing things. In the story, 'Ignorance' is represented by a starving, dreadful-looking boy.
solemn	'The Phantom was exactly as it had been, but he dreaded that he saw new meaning in its solemn shape.'	Serious; intense.
solitary	'(Scrooge was) secret, and self-contained, and solitary as an oyster.'	Lonely
want	'This girl is Want' & '(Christmas) is a time, of all others, when Want is keenly felt, and Abundance rejoices.'	Needing or desiring things. In the story, 'Want' is represented by a starving, dreadful-looking girl.

A Christmas Carol: A Graphic Revision Guide for GCSE English Literature

Vocabulary: things & objects

THE POOR LAW

A law passed in 1834 that was meant to help poor people by putting them in school or workhouses.

WORKHOUSES

Large buildings where poor people were sent to live if they didn't have a job or home. The work here was hard, the food was bad, and families were split up.

COUNTING - HOUSE

An office where accountants worked.

SHILLING

A coin that is around the same value as £4 today.

EXTINGUISHER CAP

'Extinguish' means to put out a flame, so the Ghost of Christmas Past's 'extinguisher-cap' can be used to 'put out' the light that comes from its head. Scrooge uses this to get rid of the ghost at the end of Stave 2.

POULTERERS'

A butcher shop selling poultry: chicken, geese, turkeys and other meat from birds.

Phantom/ Spectre

Ghost or spirit.

Who is being described?

Draw a line to match the quote to the character the quote describes.

he is the pleasantest-spoken gentleman you ever heard

Always a delicate creature, whom a breath might have withered.... But she had a large heart!

He has the power to render us happy or unhappy; to make our service light or burdensome; a pleasure or a toil.

an odious, stingy, hard, unfeeling man

As good as gold...and better.

a fair young girl in a mourning-dress: in whose eyes there were tears

A Christmas Carol: A Graphic Revision Guide for GCSE English Literature

Which place is being described?

Draw lines to show which place is being described.

'a mansion of dull red brick, with a little weathercock-surmounted cupola, on the roof, and a bell hanging in it. It was a large house, but one of broken fortunes; for the spacious offices were little used, their walls were damp and mossy, their windows broken, and their gates decayed.'

The graveyard from the future

'they were now in the busy thoroughfares of a city, where shadowy passengers passed and repassed; where shadowy carts and coaches battled for the way, and all the strife and tumult of a real city were.'

Scrooge's old school

'Far in this den of infamous resort, there was a low-browed, beetling shop, below a pent-house roof, where iron, old rags, bottles, bones, and greasy offal, were bought.'

Old Joe's shop

'It was a worthy place. Walled in by houses: overrun by grass and weeds, the growth of the vegetation's death, not life; choked up with too much burying; fat with repleted appetite.'

The moor

'monstrous masses of rude stone were cast about, as though it were the burial-place of giants; and water spread itself wheresoever it listed, or would have done so, but for the frost that held it prisoner; and nothing grew but moss and furze, and coarse rank grass.'

The warehouse where Scrooge was an apprentice

Who said it?

Match the quote to the character who said it:.

> Mankind was my business. The common welfare was my business; charity, mercy, forbearance, and benevolence, were, all, my business.

> What!...would you so soon put out, with worldly hands, the light I give?

> (Father) spoke so gently to me one dear night when I was going to bed, that I was not afraid to ask him once more if you might come home; and he said Yes, you should; and sent me in a coach to bring you.

> I am sure I have always thought of Christmas time...as a good time; a kind, forgiving, charitable, pleasant time.

> He frightened every one away from him when he was alive, to profit us when he was dead! Ha, ha, ha!

> I am as light as a feather, I am as happy as an angel, I am as merry as a schoolboy.... A merry Christmas to everybody!

A Christmas Carol: A Graphic Revision Guide for GCSE English Literature

How would you feel if...

You had to spend all of your time at school and could not go home much, even when all of your friends did? *(happens to young Scrooge, Stave 2)*

You worked for a person who was mean to you, didn't pay you enough, and would not even let you stay warm at work? *(happens to Bob Cratchit)*

You had to live as an unhappy spirit, dragging chains around for eternity because you did not live your life well enough? *(happens to Marley's Ghost, Stave 1)*

You kept inviting someone to spend time with you at Christmas, but they rudely refused every time? *(happens to Fred, Stave 1)*

The person you were going to marry starts caring less about you and more about making money? *(happens to Belle, Stave 2)*

You learned that some of the things you did in the past were unkind and unpleasant, but you were given a chance to change and live life positively? *(happens to Scrooge)*

TRUMP CARDS

Give the characters a mark out of 10 for each quality listed on the card. 'Wealth' means how rich they are; 'happiness' is how happy they are; 'loneliness' is how alone they are; 'love of Christmas' means how much the character loves Christmas, and 'generosity' is how much they consider and share things with other people.

Scrooge (Stave 1)

Wealth . . . .
Happiness . . . .
Love of Christmas . . . . .
Loneliness . . . .
Generosity . . . .

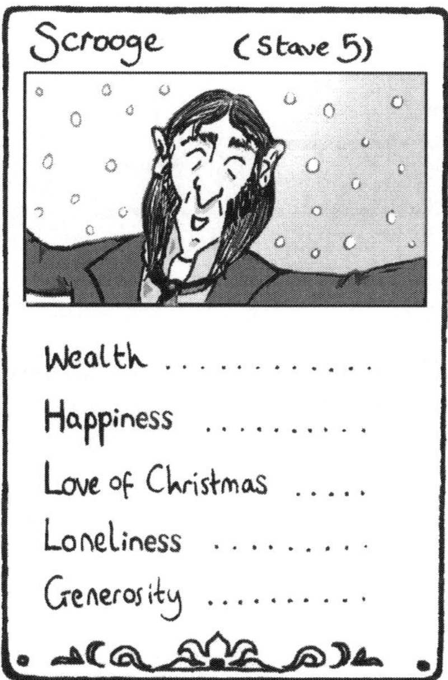

Scrooge (Stave 5)

Wealth . . . .
Happiness . . . .
Love of Christmas . . . . .
Loneliness . . . .
Generosity . . . .

Bob

Wealth . . . .
Happiness . . . .
Love of Christmas . . . . .
Loneliness . . . .
Generosity . . . .

Tiny Tim

Wealth . . . .
Happiness . . . .
Love of Christmas . . . . .
Loneliness . . . .
Generosity . . . .

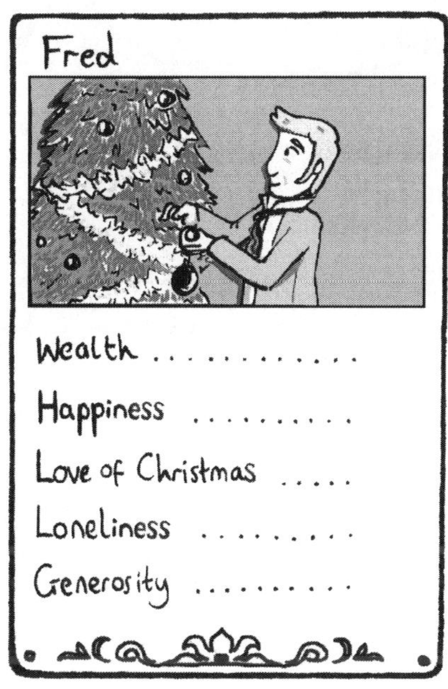

Fred

Wealth . . . .
Happiness . . . .
Love of Christmas . . . . .
Loneliness . . . .
Generosity . . . .

Fezziwig

Wealth . . . .
Happiness . . . .
Love of Christmas . . . . .
Loneliness . . . .
Generosity . . . .

A Christmas Carol: A Graphic Revision Guide for GCSE English Literature

Find an important quote said by this character: Find an important quote about this character:

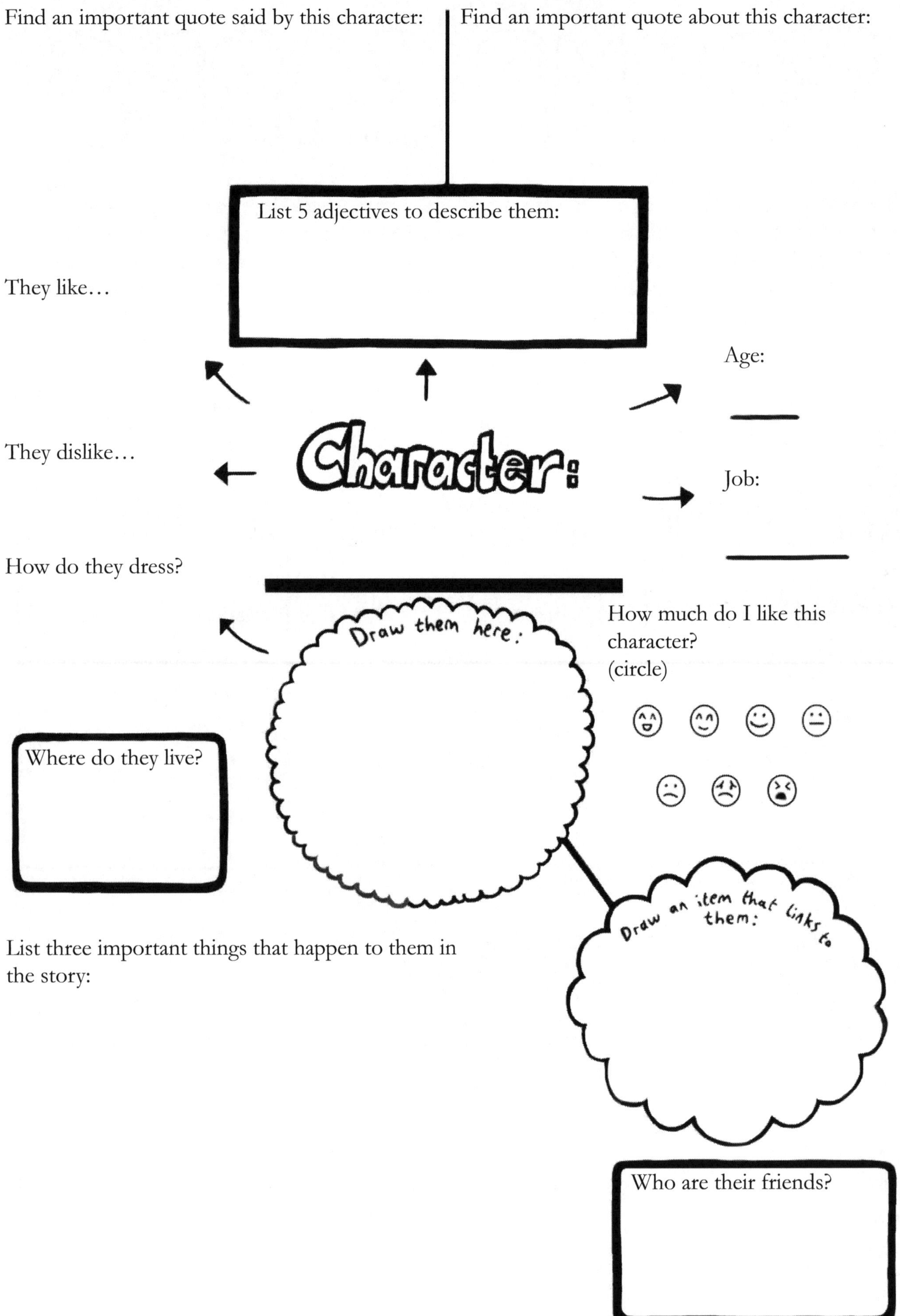

QUOTE ANALYSIS

Chapter: Page: Said by:

Language techniques:

Key words:

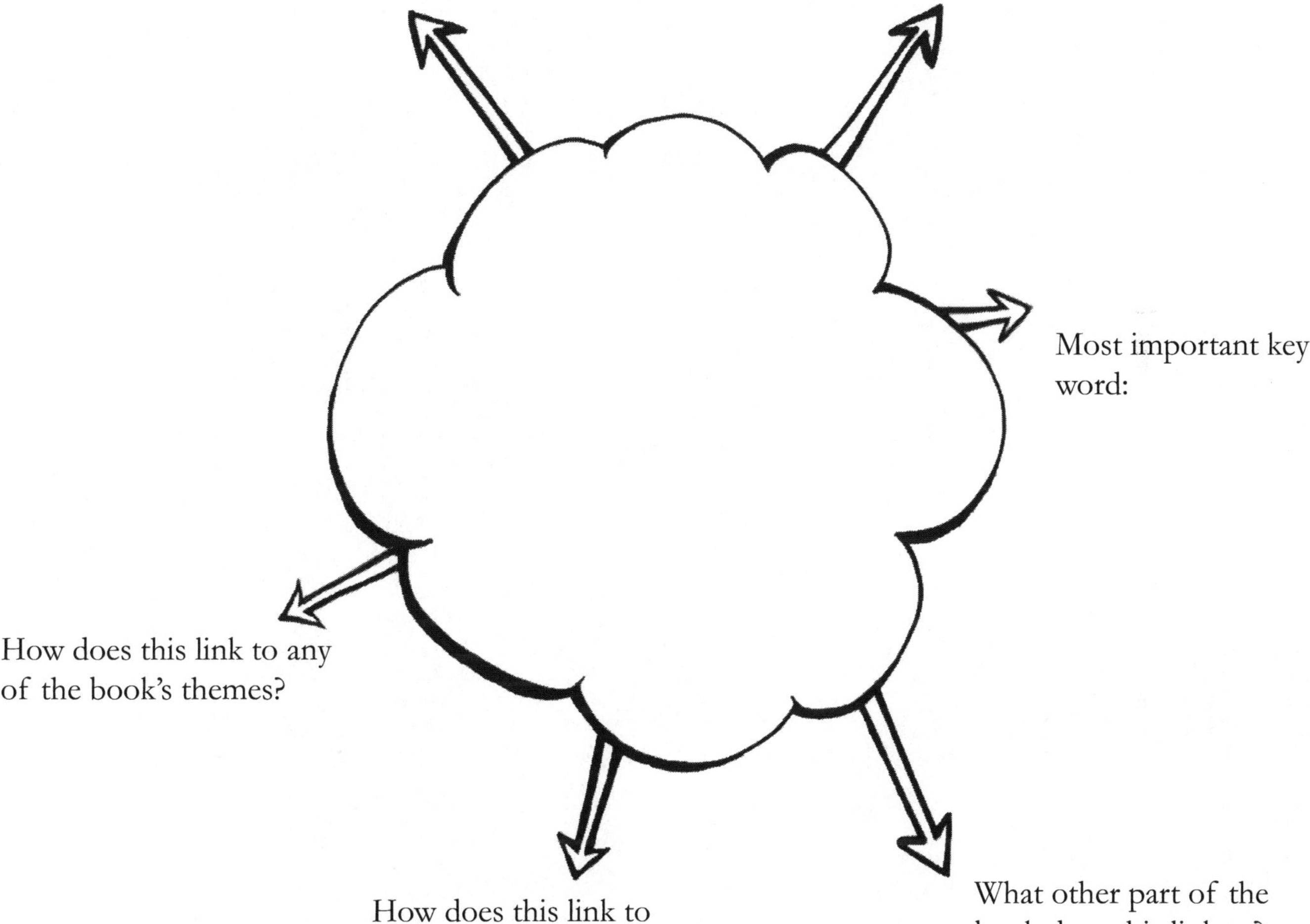

Most important key word:

How does this link to any of the book's themes?

How does this link to the context?

What other part of the book does this link to?

A Christmas Carol: A Graphic Revision Guide for GCSE English Literature

Printed and bound by CPI Group (UK) Ltd, Croydon, CR0 4YY

05/06/2026

02129288-0002